Astral Tribal

Poems and Epics

by *Journey*

Introduction by E. Nina Jay

PUBLISHER | **Verbanizm** Ink

Copyright © 2019 by **Journey**

All rights reserved. No part of this publication may be reproduced, distributed or transmitted in any form or by any means, without prior written permission.

Publisher| **Verbanizm Ink**
Cover Painting| **Jaha Zainabu**
Cover Design| **Journey**
Photographer| **Kim Roseberry**

Publisher's Note: This is a work of fiction. Names, characters, places, and incidents are a product of the author's imagination. Locales and public names are sometimes used for atmospheric purposes. Any resemblance to actual people, living or dead, or to businesses, companies, events, institutions, or locales is completely coincidental.

Astral Tribal: Poems and Epics/ Journey. -- 1st ed.
ISBN 978-0-9899300-0-0

For Us

**Introduction by
Poet|Painter|Activist
E. Nina Jay**

*I want to run
But am trapped by the cracks
In caged thought*

*I want to talk
I want to scream
Silently into the
Solace of solitude*

*But my voice can't find
The fortitude to push passed
The ghost in my throat
And I choke on the sound
Of bit tongues*

The sirens are crying.

Make no mistake… I am biased. I do not walk in as a stranger who has just read Journey's work for the first time and wish to present her to you like some strange, beautiful plant one might happen upon while hiking a rugged mountainside. This is not to say she is not strange and she is not beautiful. She is both.

Strange, like how did she write herself inside my psyche, and rearrange my thoughts this way? Beautiful, like how did she write herself inside my body, and touch n move my emotions this way?

I have been reading and falling in love with Journey's poetry for more than a decade. Her poetry has been my muse, my liberation, my safe space and a deep ocean wherein I have immersed myself to keep from dying emotional, artistic and spiritual deaths. When I could not find my own words, her poetry has been the breath I needed.

I became entranced by her poetry online, wondering "who is this womon, who writes my soul, my life, in such a way?" This led me to purchase her first book *Necessary Journey: A Collection of Poetic Injections*. I was blown away by her work and I've been hooked ever since.

I have been waiting on another book from her for many years, which is why I was absolutely humbled and overjoyed that she asked me to write an introduction for a new collection of work.

Astral Tribal is an invitation into a world of powerful imagery and mind blowing language. The work has bite and chew and swallow.

As I've stated, *Astral Tribal* is the 2nd volume to come from this writer and having read both, I can say that Journey's writing takes its place among the Audre Lordes, the Toni Morrisons, the Pat Parkers, in my life. This book took my hand and ushered me along a winding journey of thought and emotion.

Her truth is sensitive and unflinching:

Said the child to the mother
I saw you high and a star fell
From my sky

Said the addict to the child
Close the door behind you.

Her compassion and intuition create a path for me to walk into rooms that frightened me previously. There are entire stories told in her poems. Stories that have lived a very long time without sound. Stories that have no beginning and no end. Only intensity. Only certainty.

Astral Tribal is the work of generations. Journey is a poet/writer who, I believe, has lived many lifetimes, and collected many stories to be told. Her words invoke the great grandmother, the grandmother, the mother, and the child. Once you begin to open yourself to her words, you realize very quickly that you are listening to either a very old womon or a womon who does not live her entire life, on this earth, in this time or in her body. She exists elsewhere, her writing hints to me. Her wisdom and range of emotions are ethereal.

I have always told her, as I'm sure many have, that her name is perfectly chosen. I journey through her portals using winding roads made of words through the dark of her brightly lit planets. I know. but I cannot be dramatic enough. She is made of planets. Different worlds with different ways and different voices, changing from page to page. Lifetime to lifetime. Planet to planet. Yesterday to beyond tomorrow.

I kiss the foreheads of my children
Smearing the stench of petroleum across
Their future memories.

A native of the islands of Hawaii, she is a daughter to Queen Liliʻuokalani. Living in the black skin of her enslaved ancestors, she is a daughter to Harriet Tubman. Both their lives can be found in the bold pain, rage, resiliency, and strength of her words. Her work is quiet and calculating. She observes the world and every single detail in it. She is an investigator. A reporter. A griot. She led me down roads in Astral Tribal that I was afraid to walk and managed to do so in ways that left me devastated and comforted. At the same time. Enraged and joyful. At the same time.

In the ghettos. In the slums and
Barrios. On the homesteads and
Reservations. We don't take no
Vay-kay-shunz

We be too busy breathin'

Uncompromising. Bold. Intense. Beautiful. Painful. A truth that cannot be hidden from. She does not seek to make it look pretty or make it palatable. She is a screaming, crying, fighting black warrior, attempting to grasp clarity of the world of our mothers lived, and create a blueprint for herself and her children. To make sense of a world that does not make sense. Her words mark her a fighter for black n brown children who no longer live and also those who have not yet been born.

It was the bones, what did it
How they caved
Crumbling like ruins
Of fallen empires.

She cries for yesterday and screams for tomorrow. She speaks strongly for today

They love our athletes
But do not love our lives

White rage. Black scars
Drip tear onto pavement
March blood up barrel
Shoot self-inflicted noose
Hands cuffed into back

They love our music
But do not love our lives.

Journey dissects the audacity and consequence of colonialism in ways that seduce the gaze out of academic text/research and prop it against the many actual lands and lives it interrupts and alters. There are granules of sand and tiny island footprints running across the pages of her poetry.

Hawaiian bloodline
Drowned out in blackwash
Of a faceless father

Astral Tribal pulls you away from the television, which has trained us to believe that the danger we live in is natural. That the injustices we face are normal. That the indignities we suffer should be expected.

Astral Tribal intimately allows you entrance into the black home, as a black mother tries to keep a steady voice as she talks to her black son, in an effort to keep him alive in a world that continues to hunt him like wild boar…

It's a system

They'll check for warrants
Prepare a place for you
Among the chattel

Arrange your transportation
Through the complex of
Industrialized prisons

Where the rest of your kindred
Collect like interest in the
Accounts of white babies

Her ability to grab hold of a fleeting moment and paint the picture of the story with meaning, while using very few words, is unmatched by many.

You might get the feeling, as you read, that this womon has stood on the edge of death many times. Like a cliff. And that she has often thought of jumping but something bigger, living inside her, snatches her back each time. I can only imagine that something bigger has sometimes been the poetry that is her soul, begging itself to be written. begging her to live and do battle with the silences...

Flailing from your tonsils
Banging desperately on the
Back of your tongue pleading
Scream, damn you!!

Astral Tribal rises out of the desert of her quiet like a mountain of moving sand. I climb and I climb and I climb. And all I want to do is climb...

And he
Whose wings bring no flight
Has lost his sting

Somewhere & sometime ago
Buried it deep in some hole called
Woman

She brilliantly intersects what many treat like theoretical struggles, with the everyday movement of life, which is how they must be lived. And survived. And her words tell the story of that dichotomy in a way that is gut-wrenching and mesmerizingly beautiful, at the same time and using the same words. Her ability to do that, in her way is nothing short of magical to me.

Chicago, Illinois
Sept 11, 2019

Table of Contents

I

1. Spin — 16
2. The Water This Time — 17
3. Sovereign — 20
4. The Door — 22
5. Loop — 23
6. Unmemory — 25
7. Fog — 27
8. Only Notion — 30
9. Santa Claus Blue — 31
10. Glass Lakes — 33
11. All Who Wander — 35

II

1. Remind Me to Tell You — 40
2. Ripple — 42
3. Residual — 43
4. Unspeak — 46
5. Go Home. You're Dead — 48
6. Pockets — 50
7. Wind Carver — 52
8. Edge of Bone — 54
9. Processed — 56
10. Warning Label — 58

III

1.	Oasis	60
2.	Popolo	62
3.	The Good Friend	64
4.	Songs (A Spoken Blue)	66
5.	Once	69
6.	Breach	70
7.	Paper Bridges	74
8.	A Curious Thing	75
9.	Sticks & Stones	77
10.	Kept Company	79
11.	Breathe	81
12.	Us	82
13.	Ordinary	84

IV

1.	Gutterfly Soul	86
2.	The Verdict	92
3.	Beekeeper	97
4.	Siren Cry	102
5.	Pictures in a Long Green Hallway	108
6.	Mary	124
7.	She Was	131
8.	Hang Up	139
9.	Astral Tribal	150

V

Glossary

I

Spin

No one wants
To walk this road
Alone

All these ghosts
All this blood
All this anger

Looking like love.

The Water This Time

T|here are dead seas scrolling
Through my Aquafina
The water this time will not quench

Will not rise like bitch's tongue
To lick the feet of beings made niggers
By so black white flag pleading salvation
From an iron god with a
Nikon on his shoulder

Breaking news- There's a dog
Up there too

I kiss the foreheads of my children
Smearing the stench of petroleum across
Their future memories

At the gas station
$50 American dollars buys me
1,000,000 tons of whale's blood
And they say we're in a recession

T|here are dead seas scrolling
Through my Aquafina
The water this time will not quench

It will swallow

::breathe::

18 by 17

::breathe::

15 by 17

::breathe::

14 by 13

::breathe::

Bye six.

Mercy

We bury our dead in lead coffins
Lest the debt of our deeds surface in
The middle of our cruise ship commercials

Why not?

Vacation (vay-kay-shun) n

 A period of time devoted to pleasure rest or relaxation. Especially one with pay granted to an employee

Oh.

In the ghettos. In the slums and
Barrios. On the homesteads and
Reservations. We don't take no
Vay-kay-shunz

We be too busy breathin'

::spit::

T|here are dead seas
Scrolling through my Aquafina
The water this time will not quench

It will crawl up our throats
And slit our bit tongues

It will hold our heads between
It's oily thighs and make us
Eat our last breath

I lick the ash of ancestors from
My lips and pull from them
The bones of 92 octane fish

Cry me a desert

The water this time is fire.

Sovereign

It happens at times
Shadows
Jump at sight of us.

Forgetting, I think
We also move
In and out
Of light

Forgets these faces
This flesh and bone
These mounds of moans
Cussed up from sepulchers

Sway
Creak
Like old planks
Beneath thatched roofs when
Bodies crawl to
Altar

There is no conjure in
Forgiveness. Only the
Throwing of down of chains
Belonging to ghost who've
Long lost interest in carrying
The baggage

It is us, now
Watching shadows.
They do not watch us.
As we lay, they

Move on

A darkness which
Does not suffer from
Our light complex.

The Door

Said the child to the mother,
I saw you high and a star
Fell from my sky

Said the addict to the child,
Close the door behind you.

Loop

We told our mothers
They wouldn't have to
Recycle cans no more

We told our mothers
They wouldn't have to
Sell tortillas no more

We told our mothers
They wouldn't have to
Scrub floors no more

We told our mothers
They wouldn't have to
Sell their souls no more

We told our mothers
They wouldn't have to
Beg, borrow, steal no more

We told our mothers
Everything would be alright
We said this with pride

And when they died, we

Recycled cans and
Sold tortillas and
Scrubbed floors and
Sold our souls and
Begged, borrowed, stole

To pay for their funerals.

Unmemory

Drunk with dreaming, we were
Incoherent to the world
Through which we staggered.
Wanderlust on our breath, we
Reeked of stardust
And melancholy

Arms outstretched
We held the spells of gods.
Ran we, through the temples
Blasphemous bastards
Orphaned by belief. The priest
Cursed our deliverance
As the choir sang we sweetly
To chamber of the Virgin

We were free then
No roof for our heads
We bed the cosmos.
I remember Andromeda,
Thighs thick as Milky Way.

She wrapped herself
Around my waist
But you were jealous,
So she poured herself
Across the sky and
Had us both.

We are here now,
No one sees us.

We are myths, you and I
A whispered inkling.
A forgotten remember

They will not write of us, you know?
The dreamers. They are
Strangers to themselves
And far too sane for reason.

Fog

To want to reach
Instead, recede.

To watch the petals
Of your favorite orchids
Float beyond peripheral.

To not turn head
To think it better
Dead

To inhale
To smell casket
They are burying
You

To feel satin
Against pulse

Sound of earth
Raining down
And over

Darkness swallows
Every word you
Should have said

Verbs crawl

Out from under
Pallbearer's sleeve

Pool into tear
In corner of eye

Slip
Into
Ear

To want to reach.
There is no room
To move inside
This space

Recede

To feel the salt
Inside of sweat
Bleed through

Sunday best

Your
Favorite
Color

They have
Always loved
The way Blue

Becomes you

To feel the light
Slide 'cross the deep

To sleep
To reach
And then

Recede

They
Are gathered
Here today

Save breath
For journey
Beloved
Save breath

Amen.

Only Notion

And I would forfeit next lifetime
To be at once the inhale on your tongue
And tear licked from crest of lip

If at this moment
I could ride the reverberating
Current of *I love you*

That electric river
Coursing through your throat.
A deity's meditation

I would shed
My heathen's cloak to
Kneel before your altar

The inhale on your
Tongue, the teardrop licked
From crest of lip.

Santa Claus Blue

We are
Not afraid of your
Teargas

Our eyes are
Sprayed everyday with
Images of ourselves dying
Beneath your headlines

We are
Not afraid of your
Penitentiaries

We go there
To read love letters
Written 'cross solitary confinements
By forefathers who knew
We'd come

Eventually.

Has anyone
Ever told you
Your eyes are
Santa Claus blue?

They glisten
Off the street lights

And whites of your teeth
When you kill us

We are not
Afraid of dying out
It is the dying that
Exhausts us

It's the getting up

Over and
Over and

Has anyone
Ever told you
Your eyes are
Santa Claus blue?

They shine
They really
Do.

Glass Lakes

We are
Stone swans
On glass lakes

We understand
But have not mastered
The necessity of
Smooth and steady strokes

Lest the ripples we create
Send us spiraling
Through the dark
Of a depth we have not
Capacity to comprehend

Flaunt we feathers
Of obsidian. Spellbound
By the play of light. We
Think we light

Think we other
Than sinking swans
Through glass of
Mirrored flight

So smooth
We never see the ripples

Or hear the shattering
Of stone swans through
Glass lakes.

All Who Wander

If I've ever loved you
I loved you pure
Sister, brother, friend
Stranger, even

If I ever loved you
Chances are
You never knew it
For it did not
Look like the love
In your picture book

Did not
Remind you of roses
And bubble baths
Breakfasts in bed
Or walks in park

More than likely
It passed quietly
Like bone broth
In old pots. The last
Of everything I had

Or five in your gas tank
Making past tense, history of that
Empty sign of running out

Of whatever
You thought
You had

If I ever loved you
It probably didn't taste
Like filet mignon
Or truffles

Closer to numb of wine
When you whined too much
Bout all the gardens your dreams
Promised but never grew

Like that time you
Called the constellations
By all the wrong names

Ghettofied the deities
Until they looked like
Something you could
Touch some day

If I ever loved you
It looked like rain come
Falling over angels
Felt like sun scorching
Through demons

Like fathers you never met

Mothers you only knew
Something, like you searching
For yourself, disappointed
In who you really were

If I ever loved you
And if you ever loved me, too
I never knew it because
Like you, I did not know
What love looked like

II

Remind Me to Tell You

Remind me to tell you
How my mother saved me
From my mother

Shit in diaper
Black coffee in bottle
Six months old and breathing
In a two room shanty on
Kona coffee land

Remind me to tell you
How I hated my mother
But loved my mother.

How they were sisters
Come spiraling from
Tribe of Lono

Remind me to tell you
How it doesn't matter
Who did what and why.
They are both dead
And I am breathing

In a flat

In the middle of concrete
In a land where Kona Coffee
Is the shit

Remind me to tell you
How my mother willed herself dead
How my mother survived hell and havoc
To raise the seeds she planted
And the seeds she did not

We grew

Remind me to tell you
To remind me they were human
Born from ghosts left over
From other lifetimes

Ghosts who loved me enough
To haunt me, to cradle me
To walk with me. Companions
On some road carved. Blazed
Abandoned.

Remind me to tell you
That memories are stories we
Tell ourselves long after the authors
Have left the page.

Ripple

She said
Do not try to save me
I am not drowning
I am succumbing

And with that
I watched her sink
Into the difference

Like a stone
Tired of pretending
She ever had wings.

Residual

Sometimes
Depression
Feels like apathy

Or rather
An utter inability
To feel anything at all

And sometimes
It feels

Like a thousand leagues
Of your deepest sorrows
Swelled up like fists
In the form of a lump
In your throat

Flailing from your tonsils
Banging desperately on the
Back of your tongue pleading
Scream, damn you!!

But

A thousand leagues
Of your deepest sorrows
Is the weight of

A thousand lifetimes of
Soul splitting lost
Looped

A hangman's noose
And you're six feet up
On the wrong side of dirt

And a single tear may snap
The fuck out of the only nerve
Wishing you would, motherfucker

You are
Painfully
Aware
That

Just
One
Bullet

Would stop
The breathless

Not quite deathness
In your chest. It's

A flip

Floating between
Cowardness and
Courage

And it all looks
Like apathy from the
Outside in
So--

Unspeak

I want to say something
But upward of two hundred
Girl children have been stolen
From their dreams. Raped
Like you. When you were eleven
And you are still missing

I want to tell you this thing
But injustice is passe and 'Justice
For (this week's name here)' signs are
Now made in China. And

How far is China from
The bodega? And is EBT
WTF in signed language?

I want to speak these words
But your gas light is on and payday
Is four days away. And now isn't the time
To talk to you about climate change
And bicycles and bees and shit

I think, then, maybe I should
Write. But clear-cutting forest to
Make a point is -

And yet

Bookstores are where we go
After our *Save the Trees* protest
Besides, words will not help
Your credit score

I'm sorry
Were you saying
Something?

Go Home. You're Dead

They love our money
But do not love our lives

Go home, Trayvon
You're dead
Go home, Oscar
You're dead
Go home, Michael
You're dead
Go home, Tanesha
You're-- who?

They love our athletes
But do not love our lives

White rage. Black scars
Drip tear onto pavement
March blood up barrel
Shoot self-inflicted noose
Hands cuffed into back

They love our music
But do not love our lives

Go home, they will not name you

Go home, they will not use
What your mother gave you
To line their search engines

They love our labor
But do not love our lives

Go home, they will extinguish any
Memory of you, with the perpetual
Murders of yous, until all we have of you
Are our t-shirts

They love our culture
But do not love our lives

Go home. You're dead

Pockets

Mothers carry pockets
For pain of little boy's blues
Carry cry in pit of belly
Bandaid upon tongue

Say, son, the world is heavy
And it ain't yours to carry, no
Say, son, the world is heavy
S'why you bend your knees
When you pray

Mothers carry pockets
For tears in little girl's rainbow
Carry fire in clench of fist
Open rivers 'cross the burn

Say, daughter, the world is heavy
And it ain't yours to carry, no
Say, daughter, the world is heavy
S'why you bend your knees
When you pray

Mothers carry pockets
Too small for hurt in hearts of children
Carry blows in bend of back

Swallow baby's sorrow. Throats
Thick with the unsaid

Say, Mother, the world is heavy
And it ain't yours to carry, no
Say, Mother, the world is heavy
S'why you bend your knees
When you pray.

Wind Carver

Love is a Wind Carver's tool
The unimaginative, the
Cowardy, even

Would have we
Believe we fools
We, who etch our dreams
Into neck of sky

The rain
Will wash them away!
Laugh the lonely

How will you follow
What you can't even see?!
They are beside themselves
With revelry

Over breath
Tumbling
Uncatchable
Across breadth of
Stratosphere

Every fallen star

Is a comfort to a stone
Who cannot remember
Its own orbital path

Alas, we fly
Yes, before the eyes
Who see not what they believe
Only what is. And what is
Is we

Soaring
On invisible wings
Through worlds
Transcendental

Accessible
Through Wind Carver's tool
Alone.

Edge of Bone

We swing from edge of bone
Holy men have told our stories
On the streets of St. Colette.
We were children then

We hear our names on
Tongues of savages.
Their silk ties sully the
Light beneath our
Bare feet

We smile at the smiles
Of their pity. Pity the miles
They will tread before
Drowning

Nod our approval
Of the cotton they have picked
For our offering

Spare some change, brother?
Clink
Gods bless you

How the cotton doest fall

From their leather trees

The elders have taught us well
We must speak the language of skin when
Moving through flesh vessels

We swing from edge of bone
Carrying the wind in our marrow
Flying with our eyes closed.

Processed

In a word
We were too much
For our Selves

And so we
Dismantled
Detached

Decimated
What was grand
Into granules

More easily digested
By those who could not
Stomach our potency

It worked for awhile

We became
Palatable. Delicacy
Even

So desirable
These diluted selves

We fell for our own
Product

Becoming
Pushers of delusion
Junkies of division

Shadows
Making puppets
From flesh.

Warning Label

I used my flaws
As disclaimers.

Do not fall
I can not catch you
I am broken, too.
I said this

This did not stop me
From standing beneath your ledge
From talking you down
From extending my arms
From watching you fall

From walking away
With brains on my shoes
When you read between the lines
And jumped anyway.

III

Oasis

We wander through desert
Thirst quenched by the drizzle
Of a fading cloud. Oasis is a
Rumor we cannot afford to believe in
When even camels refuse to spit

When every soul is thirsty
Thirst becomes a normality
And no longer noteworthy

I am a traveler
Like any other
Without a map
Or a compass

Lost is no crisis
When found is no
Option

In a drizzle, I meet
A fellow wanderer. Seems
Nice enough a company
To keep

I share with her the
Drops of rain stored on
My tongue

Sweetly she sips my secrets
Away with the rain. I like her
So I don't complain

When the moon rises we lie
Together. Protection from a night
So cold, the stars shoot themselves
And call it mercy

In the morning I will
Mention the oasis. I will
Read her eyes and see
If she believes in rumors

I will pray she does
Because God was a rumor
Until she sipped secrets
From my tongue when all
I had to offer were the

Remnants of a drizzle
And the trinket of
A broken compass.

Popolo[15]

Brown girl fly
Bare feet Teflon over
Sweltering swirls of
Pahoehoe[11] backdrop

Skin
Papa'a[13] under
Kona sun
Black girl run

Fling self
Catch wind
'Come hueless in
Cloak of Pacific

Saltwater sanctuary
Tides be blind. Waves
Rush over. Absorb fluidity
Of brown and black blood

Kanaka[5] glide
Through liquid empyrean
Lose black in blue
Ride current back
To Lono

Elusion ephemeral
Ohana call from reality's shore
Daylight ebbs. Salt in hair
Emerge. Climb *pali*

Be fish
Out of water
Awkward. Dodge
Different

Ehhh, Popolo!
Michael Jackson!
What, black shit?
Dynomite!

Just another day
In paradise

Hawaiian bloodline
Drowned out in blackwash
Of a faceless father.

The Good Friend

I am trying
To unslit her wrists
She's bleeding on my
Favorite sheets

Telling me
How it's going to be
When she gets to
Heaven

I wonder if she knows
There's been a recall on
Angel's wings

You can only get so high
Before the fiction causes them
To combust, sending your
Flesh back to dust

How do I tell her
I won't be at her
Funeral?

I can't stand crowds
Can take churches even less

Don't ask. It's a long story
400 years to be exact

I'm hoping she
Won't take it personal
Like I'm trying not to
Take it personal

That she
Chose me
To die on

She's bleeding
On my favorite
Sheets.

Songs (A Spoken Blue)

Used to be we
Wrote to each other's blues
Like, *oooh, you too?*

But the years go by
And the seasons end
And the scars we played to
Stay or mend. And
Was we lovers or
Was we friends
Depends

On who's who
Died that day

We be an old song, baby
A very old song

Used to be you
Caught a cold just
So my fire wouldn't
Burn you

Used to be I
Sold my soul

Just so my body
Could earn you

But the planes
They come
And the boats
They go and

In the
Earth between
There just
Grows old

Like the blues
In the bones
That we rattle
And roll

We be an
Old song, baby
A very old song

Use to be us
Ebbed and flowed
In tear of eye
Tides in bottles
Trying to stay dry

But the nights
Leave notes
And the dawns
Lose hope

And in the hang
Of our over
We find the ropes

Slipping knots
Through the ghost
Broke loose
In our throats

Like old songs, baby

We be an old song, baby
A very old song. We just
Can't get out of our heads.

Once

I will love you once
This lifetime. It will be pure
It will be free.

Breach

Frankly speaking
I can hold you but
I cannot hold you
Together

Not right now

Not as these pools of blood
Ripple like riptides snatched
From lost lives. I've
Never been so bloody

Never been so boldly
Walking upright over chalk lines
Do they still use chalk?
Or is it dry erase now?

How clever
Much cleaner
No residue

To be honest
Me hugging you is just me
Using you for a crutch
Lest I fold

A love note read
Though never written.
Only longed for

I am ashamed to say
These poems no longer
Make glue.

They cannot stitch
There is no needle
For this string of words

I said get off me!

Your burden is too heavy
Your fear is too heavy
Your rage is too heavy
Your pain is too heavy
Our skin is

Just
Too
Fuckin
Heavy

For my thoughts right now

I

Want to dreams of rainbows
And forests of ancestors making magic
But there you go

Getting yourself killed again
And again
And

I could be next

You ever think about that?

Last night
I thought about what you thought
While you lay dying

Did you know you were
About to be dead?
Were you scared?
I was petrified. I was

Dying scared the fuck out of me. I mean
I don't know what I thought it'd be like
Sure as hell didn't expect to know
Death was what was happening.

I'm sorry if you were scared
I'm still scared

Truth be told
I used to think these arms sanctuary
But the evil came anyway

Walked right on in
Like a warm smile
Smelling like a sunny day
Feeling like a shoulder
To cry on

I said I am breaking

And I ain't asking you to save me
So don't you come falling apart
On my front porch

And I hate it has to be this way
All this lovin' done got us killed.

Paper Bridges

Loving you is half the battle
Go down Jesus, tell Moses come
And quell this raging sea between us
So I can hold you in my arms

Hating you is twice the struggle
Om mani padme hum[17]
Can't peace through this wall between us
To ever hold you in my arms

Paper bridges burn behind us
There're ashes on our walking shoes
The drums swung back and beat the drummer
They whisper in our talking blues

Om mani padme hum
Om mani padme hum.

A Curious Thing

A curious thing
This thing called Love.
It knows exactly where
It does not belong

Yet it lingers
Languid as an Indian summer
Praised for its warmth
Cursed for its heat

Ever notice
One never notices
That Love is gone until
That first snow falls

And falls
And falls

Funny how it falls

Sort of like

In Love.
It drifts
It floats

Gets carried   *away*
By subtle breeze or
Rushing gust. A

Little like
In lust but
Closer to
In love

How beautiful the sight
Of that first winter's snow
Bidding summer's heat farewell
Just after the fall

Magical it seems
The dreamlike change in season
Until curiously
The thing we notice most

Is how very cold
We are.

Sticks & Stones

Sticks & stones
But that's not what killed her
It was the audacity

It was mirror's
Backhand slam into
Fleshed reflection
It was the dereliction

It was the distorted portions
Of skin and sin and
Sin of skin

It was the bones, what did it
How they caved
Crumbling like ruins
Of fallen empires

Beneath heaving tongues
Heavy with the hatred
Of self incrimination

Fragments dispersed like birth
In the aftermath of
Precalculated death

It was the scars, no doubt
That, and the nerve

Mind you the marrow
Had barely cooled when
The memories came crawling

Spiraling spiders from
Cracks in facade

It was the names that nailed it
Coffin splintered in the thrust
Of pronunciation

Better that
Than the truth
It only hurts

Headstones
Though wordy
Never mention
The sticks & stones

But, oh
If they
Did.

Kept Company

I read until the words blurred
And when I could read no longer
I looked at the pictures until the colors bled
And when the pixels ceased to register

I said ok to the Darkness
Quietly waiting its turn
For my attention
Ok, I said

Come in
Have a seat
What is it that you are needing
From me?

Just a little of your time, it said
Just a little of your mind. Not much
Just enough to acknowledge me
That way you do the Light

Ok, I said. Ok
And we sat there
Darkness and me
In the quiet

And it laid its head in my lap
And I caressed its temple
And I loved it as I love my self
And held it like I hold the light

Tenderly
Respectfully
Loosely enough to let it move
Freely.

Breathe

Because even a
Flawed star shines light
Upon a darkened path. Reach

Because even a
Broken wing remembers
What it's like to fly. Try

Because even an
Injured heart beats in rhythm
To a purpose. Live

Because even the
Loneliest soul can heal
A wounded mass. Believe

Because even this
Moment is proof that you are
Worthy of life. Breathe

Us

Us don't give cuz we rich
Us give cuz we be rememberin'
What it's like to have nothin'
Ain't nothin' like havin' nothin

Us don't give to get back
Us give now for back
When we ain't
Have it to give

Us give you
Cuz we be you
Jus' yesterday
And maybe
Tomorrow

Us don't laugh cuz its funny
Us laugh cuz we spent our tears
And what is laughter
But spent up tears?

Us laugh and us laugh til
The tears get full again

Us tip good

Cuz us taste yo sweat
On our plates.
And us know hungry
In pot of food

Us hug tight
Hold strong
Keep we from
Fallin' down

Us know down
Know blues
Know you
Be us

In used shoes
Passed around
And around

Like miles
Like mercy
Like that.

Ordinary

We are imperfect
That is the magic of us

We line our cracks
With soot and stardust. Ink
We plug our holes
With dreams and sweat. Cumulus

Drown the sound of breaking
With laughter and loud talk. Moans

There are wands in our tongues
We speak cha cha from chaos
And two step to the crescendo
Of our own alchemy

We are imperfect
That is the magic of us

IV
Epics

Gutterfly Soul

Gutterfly soul
Ghetto staccato stretched Congo
'Cross tenement sky

Blues tattooed smooth
Onto wings tucked incognito
Into back pockets

Next to bus pass. Pen.
Text of X and Shakur. Lorde
Corner stored apparition in
Transition. Heir apparent to
Struggle's throne

Gutterfly Soul
Black thoughts entangled
In roots resistant to sorrow as
Nam myoho renge kyo[16]

Nag Champa afro
Erupting ebony over eyes
Brown as earth; set like suns
Into oceans of storms simmering
Slow below mellow mood

Aura blue. Temper, torrid as
Summer spent wildin' to sirens
Signaling contractions of troubles
To come. Come nightfall, Spirits call
Home this gutter girl.

Gutterfly Soul
Keeps pearls. On her. Tongue. Rings
In her. Ear. Drums. To her. Off. Beats
Through her. Creased. Sheets. Beneath
Linked leaked between ink stained fingers

Masterpieces penned to paint fumes
In rented rooms, cocoons resume the art
Of evolution. Griot graffitis hieroglyphic
Transcripts too ancient for stoned ages

Shades closed, ghetto walls
Fall away. Wings span expanse of
Squared space rounded
Up to 11th powers

Incense burn through midnight hours
Shadows, savage, seduce candles into
Rampant dances

Flames lick at tips of
Thoughts on verge of becoming
On purge of the numbing.

Submerged in succumbing

Incubus
Succubus
Omnipotent
Coming

Gutterfly soul
Woman. Conjur. Smoke
Herbs. Men. Roots. Deep
Trance. Back

Back, back.

Before streets cracked
Before black death in white sacks left
Blacks stacked like 8-tracks in age
Of scratched wax

Back, back.

Before black cats
Strapped black gats to black pride

To feed black bellies and
Keep black bars off
Black backs

Past that

Back before black mask
Shot black blast through black mass
To snatch Malcolm from free, Black

Go back.

Before Hamer, back
Before Chisholm, back.
Before Pro Black

Before black fruit crashed
From green trees onto
Red grass, back.

That back.

Before Buffalos Soldiered, back
Before Nat, back. Before Harriet, back
Before Frederick, back.
Black before Maroon, back.

Way black.

Before whips lashed. Before
Ships packed. Before beast tracked
Free black snatched from river's laugh
Turned cries at slave's back.
Beyond black

Back to hen scratching continents
From brown dirt
Under yellow sun in red horizons

Bleeding beneath
White moon springing black birth
To walk upright on green earth.

Back to Lucy back.
Undisputed fact
Of black first.

Gutterfly soul
Trapped mind burst free
From black thirst. Wings
Wild as winds whispering
Whims of original sins

Brown skin
Soaked in sweat of breath
Taking itself away

Gutterfly soul
Fly, girl. Shango
Sucking at her breast. Oshun
Rhythmic in her throat

Chanting down Oludumare
To rise like life between
Her thighs

Ancients march through arch of back
Back to river's laugh. Bridging gap of
Village past and tenement glass

Blood of sacrificial life spans drip
Crimson visions clear as tears rolling
Over ecstasy's lips and onto
Fluttering wings of

Gutterfly Soul
Ghetto staccato stretched Congo
'Cross tenement sky.

The Verdict

The night of the verdict
My twelve year old son brought
Tissue for my tears

As we sat in the
Quiet of quarters
Time lapsed

Swallow shame of
Mother unable to promise her
Child's next breath

Hear the hounds snap
Speak softly
Channel rage

Sethy,
Your black is beautiful, baby
Don't let them tell you different
But listen, this is what it is

Slavery

Carry yourself
Taller than anybody else

Speak. Clearer
Than anyone else
Be smarter than
Yourself

Keep your papers in order
Because the moment you step
Off the plantation of compliance
They'll come for you

Keep your grades up
Keep your money in the bank
And your bank card at the ready

Money is momentary
But sometimes a moment
Is all you need

Keep your insurance
And registration in arms reach
When you drive.

Keep alcohol off your breath
And drugs from your blood
Because when they pull you over

And they will

They'll test you

Make you breathe into tube
Make you touch your nose
Walk a straight line

Ask where you live
Where you work
Who's your father
Where's your mother

What are you doing
With no master present?

They'll feel you up
Check the threat between your legs
Run their hands across your arms
Thighs. Chest

Assess the whites of your eyes
Make you stick out your tongue
Run your name through the system

It's a system

They'll check for warrants
Prepare a place for you
Among the chattel

Arrange your transportation
Through the complex of
Industrialized prisons

Where the rest of your kindred
Collect like interest in the
Accounts of white babies

Keep your clothes pressed
Keep a smile in your pocket and
A hollow point on your tongue

Be prepared to run
When the ground
You're standing on turns
Conveyor belt into
Beast belly

But when you run
Run with scissors

Break into the

Wretched cage of
Devil's ribs and cut that
Motherfucker's heart out

Hold it beating and
Bleeding above your
Matted crown

Offer it to the people
Bellies bulged from scraps
Of sanctimony

Let us be fed.

Beekeeper

World worn wings
Embrace ground. A
PostScript to day

Prey pray protection
From swarming crowd
Of neon hive

Stinging no thing in particular
Stinging. How they sting
Eachother. Themselves

Each time dying
Minuscule deaths. Ends
To minuscule lives
Lived in vain

Pincushions of pain
Sewing threadbare
Fabric of life.

Cloth never thick enough for warmth
Never thin enough to offer relief
From swelter of living hells

And he
Whose wings bring no flight
Has lost his sting

Somewhere & sometime ago
Buried it deep in some hole called
Woman

He
Who lived to tell the tale
Of the one who came to play
But lost the game

Pity, he survived

A premature footnote in lost
Volume of scribes, scrolled
Along the bottom of some
Cage called Survival

Where to go?

In a hive where fireflies
Eclipse the sun when no
One is watching?

How to dry

Eyes that cry millions
At a time?

Come nightfall
Scars cloud skies
Scraping heaven

If he could fly
He'd cut to the top of the hive
And slaughter the Queen

Bitch, is she
Engorged off cud
Of working class
Fantasies

Is it so wrong to want
Honey dripping from tips of
Fingers worked to bone
In the making?

Promises wept are
Seldom kept

There are chambers
Haunted by dreams meant
Only for the sleeping

Temporary sanity
Never meant for
The keeping

Slurred confessions
Weighted messages
Bottled and tossed
Into rivers going
Nowhere

And he knows
Where optimistic suicides
Await spider's web

Justified derelicts
Surge and recede like debris
In society ruled by half moons

Whose hue is only half true
Whose darkness is deeper
Than it's light

Whose shine only serves
To solidify silhouettes of prey
Who pray come night, that
The sun does not betray them
In the day

They
The bees
Milked
For their
Honey

Puppets

Whose strings are
Pulled behind scenes
Of the Busy

And he
Scorned and mourning
The loss of his sting,

Regrets every breath taken
Since he died for a woman before
Killing the Queen.

Siren Cry

It's like
I can see the rain falling
But I can't feel it

Somewhere
I'm bleeding
But I can't see it

The sirens are crying

I want to run
But am trapped by the cracks
In caged thought

I want to talk
I want to scream
Silently into the
Solace of solitude

But my voice can't find
The fortitude to push passed
The ghost in my throat
And I choke on the sound
Of bit tongues

The sirens are crying

I can see him. Staring
But he can't see me. See
He's not breathing

My father
I shot him
He's dead

The sirens are crying

I want to let loose
This piece
Is heavy

Like burdens of babies
Bearing the weight of fathers
Less fathers than men

The sirens are crying

His eyes, I want to close them
Stop them from accusations of temptation
But my hands are clenched in indignation
To what has begun to come undone

Index and trigger are one
Meshed like flesh entwined
In secret vortex of regret
The sirens are crying

I wanted him
To stop
On top of me
He said
I wanted him

I wanted him
To stop. Pop. Stop
Shots stop pop's breath
From breathing down
My neck

The sirens are crying

I played death
So well I died

Pushed him aside
While he slept
Crept to the door. But
Eyes spied dresser drawer

The sirens are crying

I wanted to close my eyes
But my ears wouldn't hear
It was easy

Like Sunday Mornings
When Mama went to the
House of the lord and
Left me behind on the
Devil's playground

The sirens are crying

I wanted to stop in my tracks
Backtracked to bedroom door
Never wanted anything more

The sirens are crying

Than to stop him
On top of him, I said
He wanted it

And he wanted it
That way. Me on top for a change

Strange new game in our
Arrangement

The sirens are crying

Engaging smile
So mildly arms wrap
Around waist, and the look
On his face was so
Peaceful

The sirens are crying

So peaceful, I squeeze
Freedom from iron bent
Into gun on his tongue

The sirens are crying

No. No.
Please. Don't.
Oh, but

This time the
Words are not mine
This time the words
Feel divine

Behind my back
The walls talk about me
They talk

But I can't hear them

The sirens are crying

For me.

Pictures In a Long Green Hallway

I

Picture: In a long green hallway, there are framed windows of photographs. Ancestors living on either side of lifelines line the walls on both sides of a sea green corridor. Spirits in sepia witnessing flesh and blood journeys of the here and now; eyes vigilant as sentries. There are among them:

Pictures: Of a veiled little girl in first communion dress. Yellow legs peek out at mid-shin; stockinged feet are cupped in patent leather babydoll shoes. She stands vulnerable as bloom in a large dirt yard in front of an unpainted mountain camp house. Hens scribble beneath fruiting mango tree just right of sun bleached patio where a copper hued rooster perches atop a rusting tin roof.

Of a soldier donned in the armor of youth. He, sinewy and built for peace of island life, sits shoulders broad and straight backed in crisp of army uniform. Barely twenty, he is on his way to live or die worlds away in the Korean War. His jet black hair is slicked beneath his soldier's crown. Eyes brown as coffee grounds promise his smile will break your heart.

Of a laughing couple in the bloom of youth on wedding day, descending chapel steps on feet made weightless in their rapture. The groom is dressed in military Class A's. His are fingers of a working man; they tenderly clasp the tiny hands of the day bright bride nestled in the bend of protecting his arm. Lithe, she smiles at blur of steps flying beneath her feet; the long white train of her satin gown flowing rivers behind them. The sun has kissed their rings.

Of a budding revolutionary in what would be her final dress. Defiant eyes challenge camera's shutter and she is not the first to blink. She is a rebel yell in midst of soft spoken sisters, alight with a burning will to exist unapologetically in face of gender taboos. Her's are eyes that laugh rainbows and cry kerosene tears. She is only slightly cursed by the movie star mole above her scarlet grin.

Of a sun weathered fisherman, shirtless and barefoot on the rocky shoreline of his island kingdom. Hair silver as the whitecaps of moonlit waters catching salt in ocean air. A fishing net sewn by his own hands drapes regal as a monarch's cape over his sunbaked shoulder. An infinite horizon of sea and sky spills forever before him.

Of these, there are more and then no more. Ageless spirits old as soul, ancestral reflections in the frames of windows hanging onto sea green walls. Glimpses of wisdom before it earned its name and lost its shine.

II

Picture: There are six identical doors leading to five contrasting spaces in the long green hallway. They are wooden doors the color of tamarind and stand like sentries between the hanging windows where sepia spirits look out at the souls traversing layered spaces.

The doors hold on to precious time. Behind them play the sounds of memories sacred and blasphemous.

Sounds of easy conversations flickering freely in stop-go rhythm of Pidgin[14;] English, the dialect of a people colonized but not conquered. The alchemy of languages learned and lost through blendings of blood and beliefs, crystallized in the exchanges spelled between walls.

There is the deep base cadence of dreams slipped through prayers drowned out by the roaring of an old work truck en route to realizing visions of the rich. Undertones of shrapnel in sound of paradigms being transmitted through generations. Reverbs of fretted quandaries: How to feed a dozen many mouths from a single backyard garden?

There are the tap splash tempos of teardrops falling onto cotton rooftops of pillows, absorbing agony like sea sponges in bottomless hearts. Muffled sounds of hush pushed down and back of frames lining sea green walls; secrets passed on like lineage.

And yet, hateful words from loving lips are forbidden in this place.

There are sounds of metal pots and bamboo spoons negotiating tender spaces. Spices, seductive, slide through breeze of jalousie windows, carried on the serenades of Cecilio and Kapono drifting from an old wood stereo. Sounds that sway to the smile of a woman in a thread worn lavender house dress. Sounds that stop at the thoughts of a salvaged girl child standing on a homemade footstool, learning to measure rice without a cup.

In the distance, an ember red horizon backdrops the fading white shadows of sailboats carving amethyst rivers into the arms of a deep blue sea on its way to black.

III

Picture: At one end of the long green hallway is an undulating door. It forms the end of a narrow three walled rectangle opening into a vacuum of space that is at once still as held breath and chaotic as loose thoughts. In front of the door is the salvaged child. Brown skin contrasting the yellow of her home sewn sundress. On the dress are tiny red roses on slivers of thin green stems. The roses are floating.

From a sourceless echo can be heard the thundering of tides through the whipping winds of an unseen storm. Waves, unhinged, hurl themselves at a cackling sky. Rejected, slingshot tears shatter against the jagged peaks of a lava rock coastline. Caves, hollow and haunted, wail beneath breaking points of cliffs hissing singed secrets into the tamarind dam wavering behind the shoulders the little brown girl.

The child is standing in a rising pool. Seawater seeps from beneath the door at her back and there is sand between her toes. Too tight rubber bands do not contain the blue black curls cascading over her ears in pigtail waterfalls. She is oblivious to all but the amethyst river lapping its way down the long green hallway, swallowing all the green.

She smells of Ivory soap in eucalyptus baths and Johnson's baby powder. The scent of Vicks vapor rub wafts through the line dried cotton cloth snuggly wrapped around her chest. They have been fastened with pink elephant diaper pins by tender yellow hands.

In the right hand of the salvaged child is a small stone mortar, in her left, the pestle. Tears form streams in the tidepools of eyes reddened by the salt. She is calling out soundlessly, voice muted by static noise of the space between here and after. The only god she's ever known is fading into a place beyond the reach of her prayers. The hands in the coffin are cold, and no longer hers to hold.

Picture: At the other end of the long green hallway are open passages. They are washes of shadows and light leading away from the familiarity of sepia sentries in sea green corridors, and into the approaching flow of an amethyst expanse. Spaces apart but not separate from the sacred and the blasphemous breathing between tamarind portals.

Wrapped in wash of light is the yellow legged woman whose fingers have sewn a thousand sundresses; whose hands have planted and prayed for each red rose on the dress of the little brown girl with pigtail waterfalls spilling secrets ears that make her cry.

The woman is floating.

She is dressed impossibly in a gown of gardenias; their thick sweet scent entwine with that of the deep green maile leis spiraling delicately from around her neck. Tucked behind her left ear, the dewy white petals of a plumeria peek out from pink-red center. She is golden apparition in a flood of violet light.

Made new, hers are eyes which have never seen betrayal, is a smile that has never had to hide an agony. Oh, the stories she could tell but didn't. Not of the abandonment or the abuse. Not of the hanai[3] ohana[10] on Hotel Street and the mahus[9] and sex workers who gathered her and her little sister up in their arms and wrapped them in safety. Not of the orphanage that followed. Certainly not about the rape and the caretaking of the man who violated her until the day he died. Certainly not that. No, hers was a tongue held, a story swallowed. Ho'oponopono[4], there were keikis[7] to raise.

There is a mulberry glow emanating from the depths of the brackish water springs flowing beneath her. They remind her of children flinging themselves from vines of trees; wingless dragonflies fluttering through the flicker of a summer sun, squealing and free. Innocence intoxicated with laughter even as it disappeared into the cool, sweet waters of Queens Bath down Kalapana way. Her eyes are a sky of flashbacks, she watches reels of her wedding day and the bliss of being enveloped in the protective arms of her Hawaiian knight. Vivid, too, are the wedding days of her children, and all the births and first luaus that followed. She can almost taste the crisp salted skin of Manini over campfires at sunset and the guava jelly stirred in her own kitchen. She awes at the jars of pickled mangos perfecting like wine under the tropical sun beaming down on her Hillcrest rooftop. She had all but forgotten them, but not the grateful embraces, so many loving embraces. Yes, joy had been here, too. Leagues and leagues of joy.

There is a sleepy serenity in her energy. It is of tiredness, reconciled and falling away. Weightless since the shedding of the body burdened by relentless pain of illness, she is free and ready to rest. From the window of her soul, she sees the opaque white shadow of a dove perched on the tip of an eyelash. Peaceful, she thinks. Heaven.

But then there is a quivering, a sinking in her heart as she wonders if she has healed enough souls in a world so full of sorrow. Wonders if she has dried enough tears, if she has raised enough children who were not her own. Has she forgiven enough wrongs, loved enough hate, given enough of what she didn't have to give, to be able to leave this world in peace? She prays that she has lived enough to die and be redeemed.

There is profound peace in this place.

The sound of tradewinds
Riding effervescent waves
Smells of home and-

*-salt? The ocean? **My** ocean?*

Heart stops

Yes, Kona wind

Heart skips

And the trees

Heart stops

Coconut trees.
The kind that lined the yard
On Oni Oni Street!

Heart leaps

The doctors were wrong!

Heart skips

*I **did** live to see my island again*

Heart laughs

Scent of the sugary tang
Of lilikoi water the mouths
Of memories

So long.
Been way too long.
I am home

Heart stops

Ku'u home[8]

Heart flies

Where are my children?

Heart-

Bare feet can hardly be seen through the surging river of lavender light whirling beneath her. Feeling the tranquilizing pull of unseen arms, her eyes fall on sepia spirits crystalizing spells between the portals and the walls of the long green hallway. They place they have prepared for her is ready.

She is drifting

But cries of the child at the tamarind door will not let her go peacefully. Her hanai, she is leaving too soon. Already fading to light, she strains to understand what the girl child is saying over the rushing river between them.

She is drifting

She wants to kiss away every cause behind each tear, but she cannot go beyond the amethyst banks

She is drifting

Shhh, shhh, shhh, Ku'ulei
I have come as far as I can go with you
The rest of the way is yours alone to go
Go mindfully, go bravely. Go.

She is drifting

Forgive me the wounds I have passed on
Take from me the humility of all I have endured
Take, too, the strength of the woman
All that pain has made me

She is fading

Forgive me my secrets.
What I hid from you children
Could have spared you
For then you would've known
Danger when you saw it.

She is drifting

Learn from my mistakes

She is fading

Remember the good, girl.
Live for the good. Forgive the bad
It's going to come. Let it

Take care of your hurts
So they can heal
Then, as fast as you can, girl,
Get back to the good.

She is flickering

Don't cry for me
My pain is gone, and I
Am still here. Just
Different

She is gone.

The little girl floats
Red roses on the waning river.

They swirl around the space
Her mother used to be

Alone now, she is sliver
Of a stem without a bloom
Lying beneath an
Empty frame

She is sleeping
She is dreaming an
Amethyst dream

She is losing ground
Forever behind the blur of steps
Flying beneath a fading god

She is leaving
She is on her way
To somewhere else.

IV

Picture: A coffin's lid closes over sleep of sepia eyes at the end of the long green hallway. Framed sentries tower soundlessly before the little brown girl in home sewn yellow sundress with floating red roses whose stems will not let them go. Motionless stands the child before the tamarind dam breaking at her feet.

Mary

Jezebel turned tricks
Like her mama turned tricks
Like her mama before her
Turned tricks, too

Had her singing
Motown love songs
In the still of the night
To soothe her baby's blues

Jezebel never heard a lullaby

Why, I cry every time
I think of the day
My, my, my Jezebel
Wrote me this song

Mary don't you weep, now
Mary don't you weep, now
Mary don't you weep, now hush

She prayed the Lord
My soul to keep, but the tithes
Were too steep, and she couldn't
Keep shoes on my feet.

Tried to bandage my cuts
But the wounds ran too deep

Mary don't you weep, now
Mary don't you weep, now
Mary don't you weep, now hush

A kiss on the lips
Left the drip of her tears
I could taste her demise
In the salt

But I knew it wasn't her fault
She said she wouldn't be gone long
Said she wouldn't be gone

Hindsight's 20/20
What she said was, *So long*
When she wrote me this song

Mary don't you weep, now
Mary don't you weep, now
Mary don't you weep, now hush

You, just stay in this closet
And don't make a peep

Eviction notice on the door
And you still gotta eat

So I'mma do what
I'mma do, but baby,
Please go to sleep
And try to ignore

The moans. and the grunts. and
Try not to smell
The pipes. and the blunts. and
Try not to hear
When he calls me a-

And try not to call it a trick
It's a stunt.
It's a jungle out here
I'm on a hunt, so

Mary don't you weep, now
Mary don't you weep, now
Mary don't you weep, now hush

Door creeps open
This motherfucker's
Smokin a blunt like
This shit is a game.

And I'm kinda gettin' pissed at
This John called Coltrane cuz
He's the typa nigga givin'
Good weed a bad name

And I'm tryin' not to burn
In Jezebel's flame
Cuz she's got nothin' to lose
And nothin' to gain

And the thunder of her tears
Torrential like rain
Roll like a whisper when
He says, *Bitch, call my name*

Battered and shattered by
The shadows of shame when
She realized I saw it all
No need to explain
Cuz I'd never be the same

Seeing in my future
The past from whence she came
Was a little too much
For Jezebel's brain

Sanity crept quietly

One way out on the night train.
I saw her in the morning
Writing this song in the ice
On the windowpane

Mary don't you weep, now
Mary don't you weep, now
Mary don't you weep, now hush

And my little heart beats
To the strides that she glides
Through the ice and the sleet.
And i'm clinging to life
On her sweet body heat.

And I swear I don't need no
Shoes on my feet
If she could just find a way
To keep me

Mary don't you weep, now
Mary don't you weep, now
Mary don't you-

Mama don't you weep!

Don't you lay me down
On this cold concrete.
Don't you make me
Promises that you can't keep.

And don't you ever sell
Your soul on some cum
Stained sheets for me

Don't need no shoes on my feet
Don't need no shoes on my feet
Mama, don't leave-
But

Jezebel turned tricks
Like her mama, she turned tricks
Like her mama before her
Turned tricks, too.

So

Mary don't you weep, now
Mary don't you weep, now
Mary don't you weep, now hush

Cuz you got nothing but time
To hold on to

Mary don't you weep, now
Mary don't you weep

You got nothing but space
To belong to

Mary don't you weep, now
Mary don't you weep

And you got nothing to do
But be strong, boo

Yeah, Jezebel wrote me
This song.

She Was

Beautiful. She was
Brilliant. She was
Daddy's pride. Mama's dream
She was. Sixteen

Honor rolled and college-bound
Found herself in love. She was
With a boy two years her senior
Second-year senior. He was

A star. He was
The sun. He was
Finally on the right track. He was
Never looking back. He was
Occupied with stacks of grooved wax that spat
Hey Mr. DJ, play another love song. He was

But wrong turns in right places
Left spaces between them. They were
A blur. They were
Children. They were

Alone when she told him. They were
Voluntary victims of ill decisions. They were
Frightened, that night when

The beautiful child. She was
Told the occupied child. He was
That they were with child. And then
They were no more

Alone. She was
At home when she told them. She was
With baby, hoping that maybe. They'd be
The shelter in her storm. They were not

Daddy's pride became a whore
When Mama's dream imploded
Behind the door the Sun
Walked out of

A swarm. They were
Stinging like bees. They were
Killing everything. She was
Ever led to believe. They were

Screams collide.
They are. Derailed trains
Against a metamorphosing frame
Inside which a child remained
Growing

Beautiful. She was

Brilliant. She was
Innocent of sin. She was

Sinking within
The skin of a babe
Aged. Made outcast
By the burden. She was

Then the dawning. She was
To be aborted. She was
A manifested regret. She was

Never to forget the calm, warm, wet
Of the womb turned tomb. She would
Never escape. She was
To be killed. At will
Come morning. She was

Mourning. She was
Willing herself still. She was
As if stillness would make them
Forget. She was

Not but six weeks old
Before breath. She was
Not but six weeks old
Before death. She was

Six weeks old and too
Fuckin young to be
Made to pay for another's regret
With her *Life*

Trembling. She was
Assembling pleas of promises. She was
To be a good girl. She was
A good girl. She was

Drowning. She was
Violently thrashing against the tides
Of her mother's placenta. She was
Pulled into undertow of tomorrow. She was

Clawing at the caving walls. She was
Chaos. She was. Panic. She was. Until

She was still. She was
Still. She was
Still to die on the death row
Of her mother's
16 year old soul

No last meal
No last request

No first words
No first steps

Kneeling on fetal knees. She was
Reaching for umbilical cord of a god
She would never call *mama*. She was

Mama was just a baby. She was
Whose child was not a baby.. She was
There

In the frenzy and fray
Of an airless vacuum
Extracted. She was

Undistracted. She was
By the fragments. She was
Becoming. She was
Becoming. She was

Orbiting. She was
Lost planet. She was
Slipping into swirling blackhole
Of secrets. She was

Stashed into bright red
Biohazard bag. She was
Tagged-*Terminated*. She was

Tossed like filth into sterile can. She was
Tiny fingers reaching for hands. She was
Bleeding, oozing, gushing pulp. She was
Breathing breath through shallow gulp. She was

Following cries of mother's plight
Out clinic door and into night. She was
Pulling self past selves down
Long dark hallways. She was

An angel with a demon's tail. She was
Leaving trails of bloodied memories
Past doorways to bedrooms where
The flesh-blessed cursed when they spoke
Of *who*. She was

She was. There
Spilled and spreading. She was

Vocal cord bulging from broken neck. She was
Muted scream when eyes caught speck

Of reflection. She was

Hideous. She was
Unspeakable. She was

Bleeding, oozing, gushing pulp. She was
Breathing breath through shallow gulp. She was
Disgustingly distorted. Unable to contain
The rearrangement of *who*. She was

Pieces of skull fall away
From inconceivable thought

Caught by the sound of bellows
She follows stairway onto landing. She was
Standing at the foot of her mother's bed
Nearly severed head listening to cries she'd cry
If *only*. She was

A shame carried to grave. She was
A chance nobody gave. She was
Unwelcomed in this beautiful world. She was
Afraid to repulse that beautiful girl. She was

Longing so strongly
To be held but. She was
The secret no one
Could tell, so

When eyes befell on closet door. She crawled
Inside. Curled up on floor. Where. She was
Quietly kept. Forevermore. She was

She was
She was
She was.

Hang Up
(For Katrina, 9/11, and All the Sean Bells)

I

We are falling over water's edge
Wedged between hard rocks and rotting spaces
Alone we face the crowded solitude

From bottoms of haunted bottles
We watch corpse swinging
Swinging
Swing
    i
     n
      g

Chariots circle
They are vultures over
Our dead bodies

Falling
Remembering
What death does not
Forget

Let it go, they say

I say, Malcolm was just a baby
Who could not let go
Of his mama's head
When his daddy
Got lynched

Time waits for no one
Because time does not exist

Brown fist wrap 'round black bars
Doing that which does not exist
Black nights cling to white stars
Afraid of their own darkness

Who are we
Who are here?
Whose black breast nursed
White babes who loved us
Before they did not
Who learned to hate

Our song
Our skin
Our race

We are falling over water's edge

II

I pledge allegiance
To who?
To the flag
Whose flag?
Of the United States of America
Oh, *that* bitch

And to the republic
What's a republic'?
For which it stands
On whom is it standing?

One nation
Where?
Under God
Whose God?
Indivisible
Invisibly?

With liberty
Liberty?
And justice
Justice?
For all

I don't get it

Amen
A man?
Amen
What man?

III

The Man
Is posing for a photo-op
In the heartland of
A massacre

In Africa the crops
Do not grow because
The farmers
Were harvested

Over water's edge we fall
Vodun uprooted
Outcast by Judas

We are falling over water's edge

IV

911
Hello?
What's your emergency?
There are planes in my window
What kind of planes?

American
Where is your window?
In America
Where are the Americans?
In Iraq

Who is flying the planes
The President
What is he doing?
He's waving at dead people
You see dead people?
Yes

Where?
In New Orleans
How did they die?
Poor

I don't understand

They drowned of thirst
Those that didn't, got
Shot stealing food and
Burst into shame

Shame?
Yes
On you?
Yes
Of what?

Of being so black we
Had to wave white flags
Just to get on TV

Did we see you?
Yes
Where did we see you?
On the roof. In the water

Did we come to get you off the roof?
Out of the water?
No
Why not?

Because you
Thought us better
Dead

Do we see you now?
No
Why not?

Because you got tired
Of our black faces and
Chained the channel

How embarrassing
Yes

Why didn't the dead people leave?
While they were still alive, I mean
With what money?
Ahh... Gotcha

Where are the planes now?
They're crashing through my window

Where is your passport?
It's under the fire truck
Where is the fire truck?
It's under the buildings

Buildings?

Yes
How many are there?
Two. No, three.

North, South and 7
All in the east
All in the west
All on 11

Where are the firemen?
They're buried in ashes
Where are the cops?
They're shooting
Sean Bell

All of them?
Most
Why so many?
Because there are so many
Sean Bells

v

Where is the President?
He's flying the planes

Can you see him?
Yes
Are you afraid?
Yes, please send help
There's no one to send
They're all in Iraq

Where are you now?
I don't know anymore
Describe what you see
Nothing. It's too dark
Yes, you can. Try

How many fingers am I holding up?
One
Very good. Which one is it?
It's your trigger finger
Excellent. What is it doing?
Aiming for me

Exactly. Stay still
Are you afraid?
No
Stay still.

Are you bleeding?
Yes

Does it hurt?
No
Are you breathing?
No
Then you're dead

No
Yes

But I don't want to die
You should've thought about that
Before you were born black.
I'm hanging up now.

No.
Don't go. Hello?
Hello?!

VI

The number you have reached
Has been disconnected

Please hang up
And die again

Black bodies swinging

                                        Please hang up

Swing
    i
     n
      g

Check the number

                                          Please hang up

Swing
   i
  n
 g

Please hang up

       g
     n
    i
Swing

                                            Hang up

Over water's edge we f
                a
                l
                l

Hang up

                       The line has been cut
              Hang up.

Astral Tribal

Ua mau ke ea o ka aina i ka pono[18]
Ua mau ke ea o ka aina i ka-
Hush, mama, talk to me
Ua- Nam myoho renge[16]*-*

Tell me how it used to be
O kai aina- in the water
I ka pono- in the water, listen
Nam myoho renge-

Somebody came and troubled
The water

We are children
Made lesser by the odds
Against our will

To be peace
To be love
To be free

We have been
The very mountain top

We are monks
In flesh and bone
Temples

*Go down, go down, children
Catch up, catch up, catch up*

We are warriors on the path
We are streams into rivers
Into seas

We are tides ebbing from
And flowing to
Ourselves

*Ua mau ke ea o ka aina i ka-
Nam myoho renge-*

*Somebody came and troubled
The water*

We are captives
Burdened by the beast
Of wants and needs
And greed

We are Confucius
Incapacitated by
Xanax bars

We are stars
Silver lining
Chemtrail clouds

We are rebels
Without pause
We are cause
Entiendes?

We have been
To the bottom of the passage
Chained to one another
By the links in Lucy's DNA

We are roots reaching for sky
We are seeds never buried
Deep enough to disappear

We appear in pieces of dreams
Screaming our way out of
Collective amnesia

We are forest
For the trees
See me?

We are Sitting Bull
Running free on Pine Ridge
Reservation

We are reflections
Of *Ali'i* going down to
Catch up, catch up, catch up

Olodumare, Ajuba gbo gbo
Iku mbeleshe¹⁹

We are drums
In the treble of
An ancient chant

Olodumare, ibaye, ibaye tonu

We are Liliuokalani
Reaching back
For Kamehameha

Ibashe Ogun

We are Guevara
Making way
For Assata

Ibashe Imale

We are Mandela
Bending bars
For Mumia

Ibashe Omo Aiye

We are shadows
In the darkness
Of a southern swamp
Stomping north

Ibashe Onile

In us is the fire of Tutu Pele
Blazing rage through
Indigo veins

Ibashe Olokun

Birthing aina[2]
For Kanaka Maoli[6]

Replacing that
Which has been
Stolen away

Ibashe Oshetura

We are Mau Mau
In the mountains
Of the Moors

We blow Geronimo, listen
We are Night Marchers
'Cross a red dirt sky

*Go down, go down, children
Catch up, catch up, catch up*

*Ua mau ke ea o ka aina i ka pono
Ua mau ke ea o ka aina i ka-*
Hush, Mama, talk to me
Ua- Nam myoho renge-

Tell me how it used to be
O ka aina- in the water
I ka pono- in the water, listen
Ua- Nam myoho renge-

Somebody came and troubled
The water

We are peace
We are love
We are free.

V
Glossary

Words

1. **Ali'i**- In ancient times, Hawaiian royalty

2. **Aina**- Land

3. **Hanai**- Hawaiian term for the act of informal adoption. Also used to describe a person of family who has either been adopted in this manner or who has adopted in this manner.

4. **Ho'oponopono**- Forgiveness or the practice of forgiving

5. **Kanaka**- Literal meaning Person. Commonly used in reference to people native to/ born in Hawaii

6. **Kanaka Maoli**- More specifically, people or person of Hawaiian descent/blood

7. **Keiki**- Child or children

8. **Ku'u Home**- Literally meaning My Home

9. **Mahu**- Word originating in ancient Hawaii and around Polynesia for a third gendered

person, that is, neither male nor female, but both or neither. (Source: Urban Dictionary)

10. **Ohana**- Family, by blood or by close relation

11. **Pahoehoe**- Smooth and ropey type of lava

12 **Pali**: Cliff

13. **Papa'a**- Burnt

14. **Pidgin**- A grammatically simplified form or a language, used for communication between people not sharing a common language, Arises out of language conflict between speakers of other languages, (Source: Oxford)

15. **Popolo**: Black person. Sometimes used derogatorily

Terms and Phrases

16. **Nam myoho renge kyo** (Buddhist, Nichiren): Principle based on the mystic law that all human beings have the power to overcome and transform any suffering or problem.

17. **Om mani padme hum** (Buddhist): The commitment to dissolving personal impurities and attaining a higher path

Note: Both above translations are per the author's personal understanding and knowledge.

18. **Ua mau ke ea o ka aina i ka pono** (Hawaiian, Kamehameha III) The sovereignty/life of the land is perpetuated in righteousness.

This phrase was coined by Kamehameha III in 1843 upon the restoration of sovereignty of the Kingdom of Hawaii from the British after the five month occupation that came to be known as the Paulet Affair.

19. **Ifa Libation** (As shared with the author along her journey towards spiritual enlightenment)

**Olodumare, Ajuba gbo gbo
Iku embeleshe**
God, we honor you and salute the ancestors who sit at your feet in council

Olodumare, ibaye, ibaye tonu
We give praise to the owner of existence and those who made the sacrifice

Ibashe Ogun
I call upon and give praise to Ogun, the path opener

Ibashe Imale
I call upon and give praise to all the ancestors who preceed the births of those who come into the world

Ibashe Omo Aiye
I call upon and give praise to the children of the world

Ibashe Onile
I call upon and give praise to the Earth which supports us and the ancestors who support us as we walk through the world.

Ibashe Olokun
I call upon and give praise to Olokun, the essence of all that comes from the sea

Ibashe Oshetura
I call upon and give praise to the messenger of all prayers.

About the Author

A native of the islands of Hawaii, Journey is a daughter to Queen Lili'uokalani living in the black skin of her enslaved ancestors; she is a daughter to Harriet Tubman. Both their lives can be found in the bold pain, rage, resiliency, and strength of her words. Her work is quiet and calculating. She observes the world and every single detail in it. She is an investigator. A reporter. A griot.

E. Nina Jay

Poet / Activist

www.ingramcontent.com/pod-product-compliance
Lightning Source LLC
Chambersburg PA
CBHW030438010526
44118CB00011B/697